# FUN FROGS/
# RANAS SALTARINAS

By Rose Carraway

Traducción al español: Eduardo Alamán

**Gareth Stevens**
Publishing

Please visit our website, www.garethstevens.com. For a free color catalog of all our high-quality books, call toll free 1-800-542-2595 or fax 1-877-542-2596.

**Library of Congress Cataloging-in-Publication Data**

Carraway, Rose.
[Fun frogs. Spanish & English]
Fun frogs = Ranas saltarinas / Rose Carraway.
    p. cm. — (Pet corner = Rincón de las mascotas)
Includes index.
ISBN 978-1-4339-6637-8 (library binding)
1. Frogs as pets—Juvenile literature. I. Title. II. Title: Ranas saltarinas.
SF459.F83C3718 2012
639.3'789—dc23

                  2011024845

First Edition

Published in 2012 by
**Gareth Stevens Publishing**
111 East 14th Street, Suite 349
New York, NY 10003

Editor: Katie Kawa
Designer: Andrea Davison-Bartolotta
Spanish Translation: Eduardo Alamán

Photo credits: Cover, pp. 1, 5 (bottom left, bottom right), 7, 11, 13, 15, 17, 19, 21, 23, 24 (crickets, skin) Shutterstock.com; p. 5 (top left, top right) iStockphoto/Thinkstock; pp. 9, 24 (tank) iStockphoto.com.

Printed in the United States of America

CPSIA compliance information: Batch #CW12GS: For further information contact Gareth Stevens, New York, New York at 1-800-542-2595.

# Contents

# Contenido

There are many kinds
of frogs.

----------------------------------------

Hay muchos tipos
de ranas.

One kind is the American green tree frog. It is the same color as grass!

---

Un tipo de rana es la rana verde de Norteamérica. ¡Esta rana es del color de la hierba!

Dwarf frogs also make good pets.
They are very small.

------------------------------------

Las ranas enanas son buenas mascotas. Son muy pequeñas.

Baby frogs are called
tadpoles.
They live in water.

------------------------------------------

A las ranas bebés se les
llama renacuajos. Los
renacuajos viven en
el agua.

A pet frog lives
in a tank.

--------------------------------

Las ranas mascotas
viven en peceras.

Some frogs are shy.
They hide in their tanks.

------------------------------------

Algunas ranas son
tímidas. Se esconden
en sus peceras.

A light goes in the tank.
This keeps a frog warm.

----------------------------------------

Las peceras tienen luces.
Las luces mantienen a
las ranas calientes.

Frogs like to hop.
This is their exercise.

----------------------------------------

A las ranas les gusta
brincar. Así hacen
ejercicio.

19

A frog does not drink water.
Water goes in its skin.

-------------------------------------

Las ranas no beben agua. El agua entra por su piel.

21

A frog eats bugs!
It likes crickets.

-------------------------------------

¡Las ranas comen
insectos! A esta rana le
gustan los grillos.

23

# Words to Know/
# Palabras que debes saber

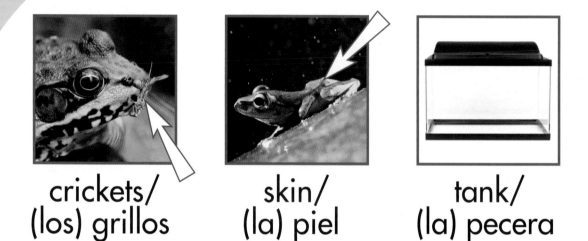

crickets/
(los) grillos

skin/
(la) piel

tank/
(la) pecera

# Index / Índice

24